RADIOHEAD

Play Along with 8 Great-Sounding Tracks

BOOK & PLAY-ALONG CDS
WITH **TNT** TONE 'N' TEMPO CHANGER

About the TNT Changer

Use the TNT software to change keys, loop playback, and mute tracks for play-along. For complete instructions, see the **TnT ReadMe.pdf** file on your enhanced CDs.

Windows users: insert a CD into your computer, double-click on My Computer, right-click on your CD drive icon, and select Explore to locate the file.

Mac users: insert a CD into your computer and double-click on the CD icon on your desktop to locate the file.

Produced by
Alfred Music Publishing Co., Inc.
P.O. Box 10003
Van Nuys, CA 91410-0003
alfred.com

Printed in USA.

ISBN-10: 0-7390-8657-X (Book & 2 CDs)
ISBN-13: 978-0-7390-8657-5 (Book & 2 CDs)

Cover image from the original Faber Music cover by The Ghost & Stanley Donwood

Contents

Drum Charts

2+2=5

Words and Music by
THOMAS YORKE, JONATHAN GREENWOOD,
COLIN GREENWOOD, EDWARD O'BRIEN and PHILIP SELWAY

2+2=5 - 5 - 1

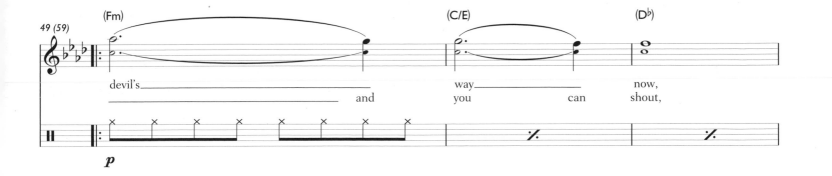

49 (59) (Fm) (C/E) (D♭)

devil's_____ and way_____ now,
_____ and you can shout,

p

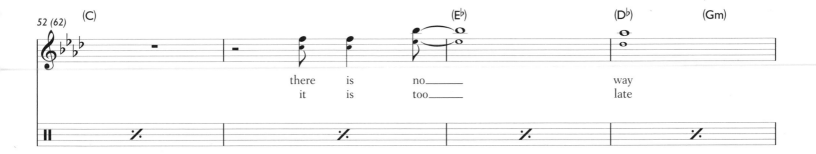

52 (62) (C) (E♭) (D♭) (Gm)

there is no_____ way
it is too_____ late

56 (66) (D♭) (Gm) (C/E) 1. 2.

out._____ You can scream,_ Be - cause___
now._____

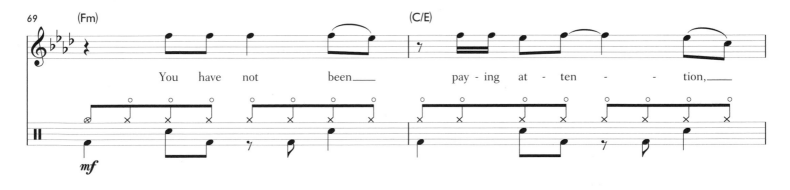

69 (Fm) (C/E)

You have not been_____ pay-ing at - ten - - tion,_____

mf

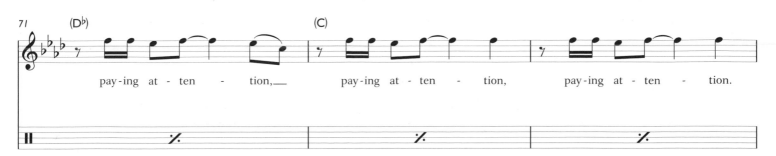

71 (D♭) (C)

pay-ing at - ten - tion,___ pay-ing at - ten - tion, pay-ing at - ten - tion.

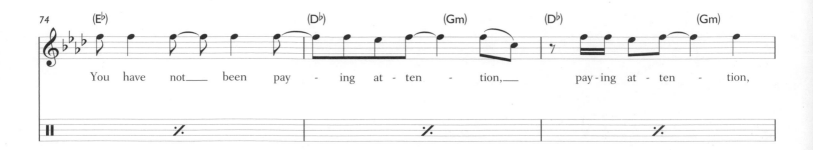

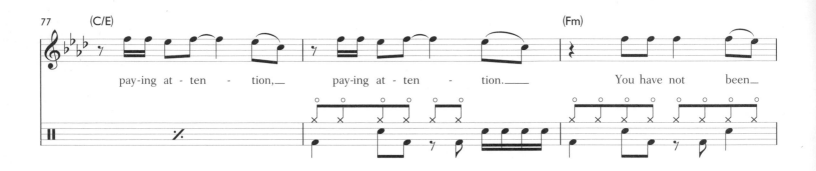

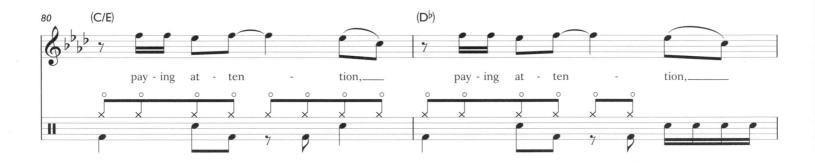

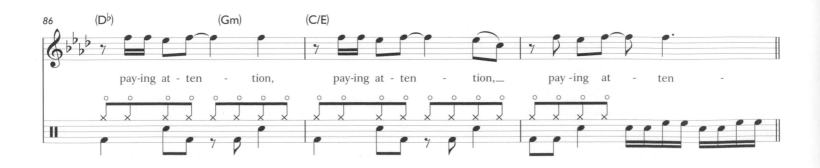

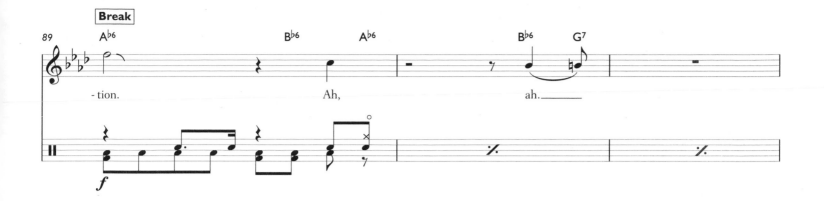

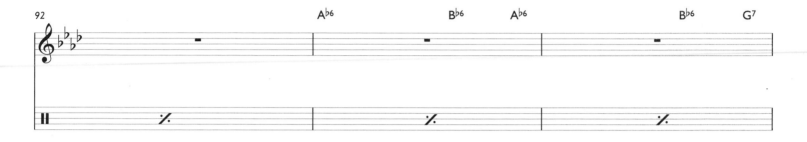

2+2=5 - 5 - 4

ANYONE CAN PLAY GUITAR

Words and Music by
THOMAS YORKE, JONATHAN GREENWOOD,
COLIN GREENWOOD, EDWARD O'BRIEN and PHILIP SELWAY

Anyone Can Play Guitar - 4 - 1

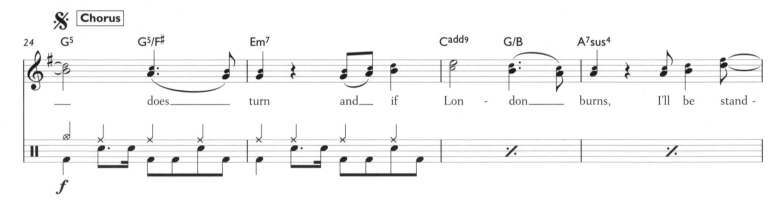

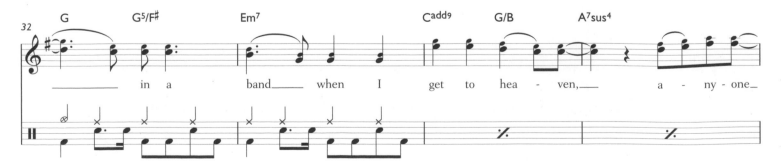

D   Cadd9   G5   G5/F#   Em   D

__ can play__ gui - tar___ and they__ won't be a no - thing a - ny - more.

Link
tempo I (♩ = 75)

To Coda ⊕

Verse 2
Em   C7

2. Grow____ my hair,__ grow my hair,__ I am__ Jim Mor-ri - son,__

splash

mp

Em

grow_____ my hair,__ I wan-na be, wan-na be wan-na be Jim Mor-ri - son.__

C7

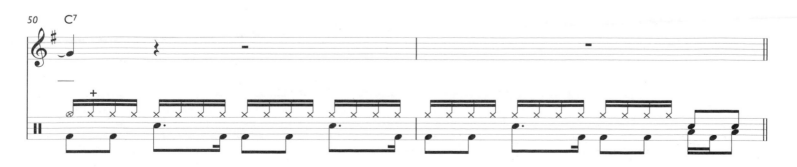

Anyone Can Play Guitar - 4 - 3

double time (♩ = 150)

52 D

Here   we are_____ with our   run-ning and   con-fu - sion,   and I don't_

56 C

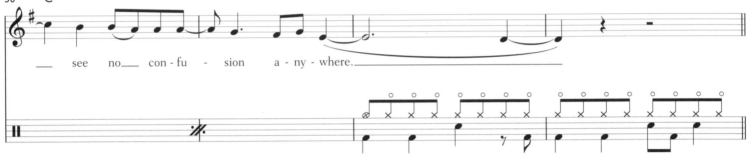

__ see   no__ con-fu - sion   a - ny - where._____

Guitar solo

60

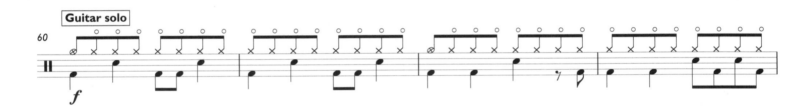

64 C   *D.% al Coda*

And   if   the   world_

⊕ *Coda* [Outro]

86

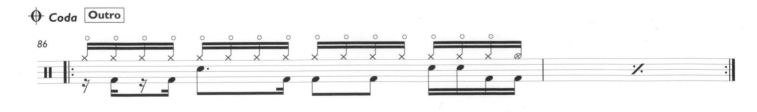

88

Anyone Can Play Guitar - 4 - 4

CREEP

Words and Music by
THOM YORKE, JONATHAN GREENWOOD,
PHILIP SELWAY, COLIN GREENWOOD, EDWARD O'BRIEN,
ALBERT HAMMOND and MIKE HAZELWOOD

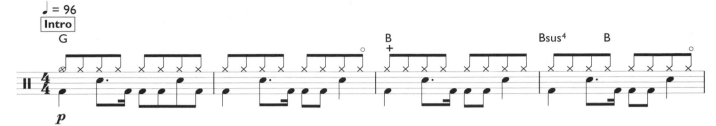

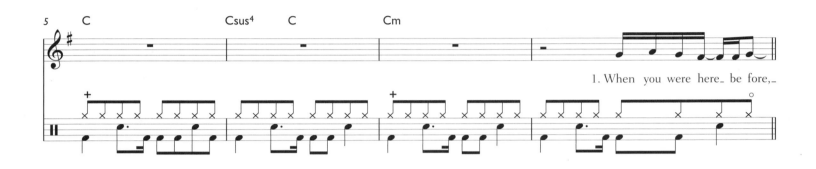

1. When you were here be fore,

could-n't look you in the eye. You're just like an an-

-gel, your skin makes me cry. You float like a fea-

Creep - 5 - 1

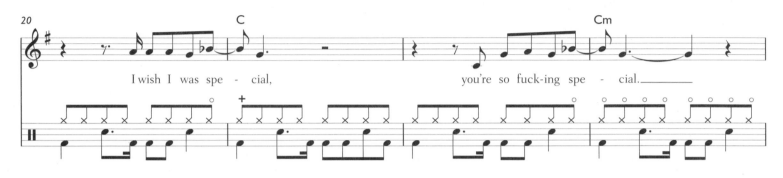

Chorus I

Verse 2

Chorus 2

Creep - 5 - 3

I don't be-long___ here.___

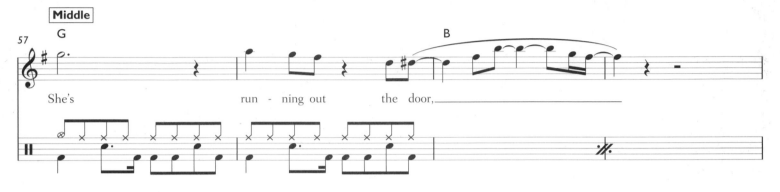

Middle

She's___ run-ning out the door,___

she's___ run-ning___ she run, run, run, run,___

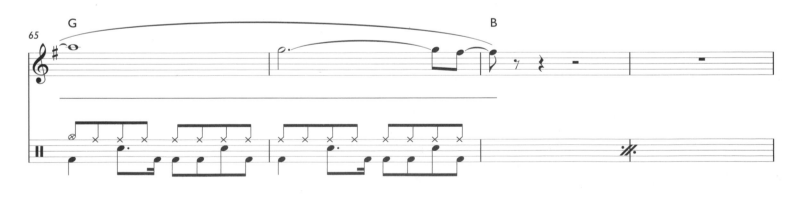

run.___ What-ev-er makes you hap-

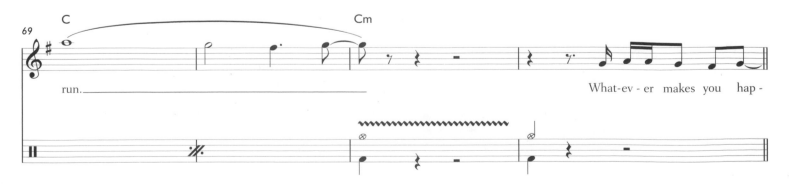

Verse 3

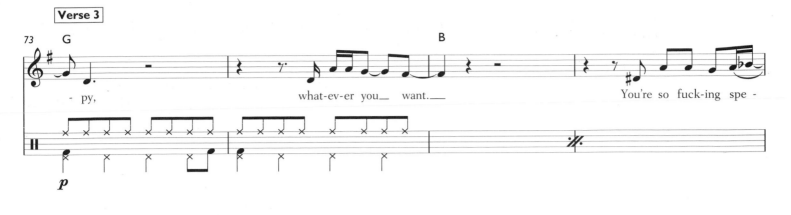

- py, what-ev-er you___ want.___ You're so fuck-ing spe -

- cial, I wish I was spe - cial, but I'm a___ creep,

Outro chorus

I'm a___ weird - o.___

What the hell am I do-ing here?___ I don't be-long___

___ here,___ I don't be-long___ here.

JUST

Words and Music by
THOMAS YORKE, JONATHAN GREENWOOD,
COLIN GREENWOOD, EDWARD O'BRIEN and PHILIP SELWAY

Just - 5 - 1

Chorus

- self,   you do,___   and that's what real - ly hurts__   is you do it to your-

- self,   just you,__   you and no - one else,__   you do it to your - self._____

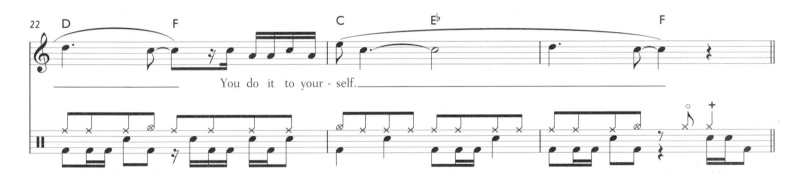

You do it to your - self._____

Verse 2

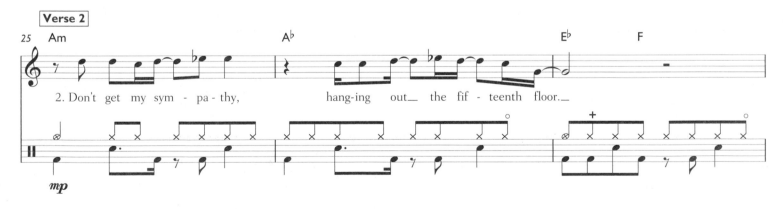

2. Don't get my sym - pa - thy,   hang-ing   out__ the fif - teenth floor.__

You've changed the locks__ three times,   he still comes reel - ing through__ the door.

And soon he'll get___ to you,

teach you how_ to get to pur - est hell. You do it to your-

Chorus 2

- self, you do,___ and that's what real - ly hurts_ is you do it to your-

- self, just you,___ you and no - one else,___ you do it to your-

- self._____ You do it to your - self._____

Guitar solo

Chorus 3

You do it to your - self,___ you do,___ that's what real-ly hurts_ is you do it to your-

- self,____ just you,_ you and no - one else,_ you do it to your-

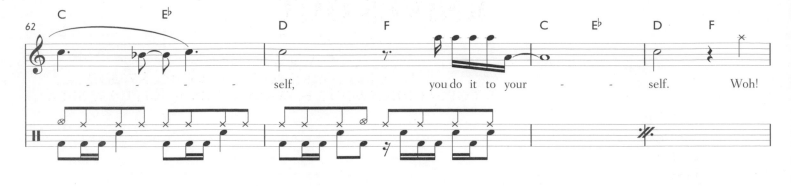

self, you do it to your - - self. Woh!

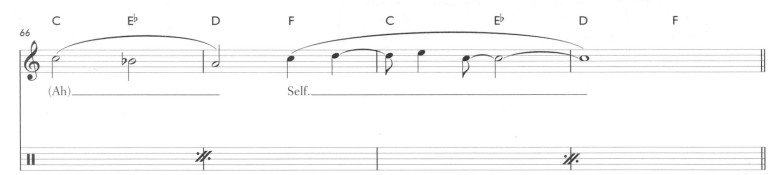

(Ah)_____ Self._____

Outro

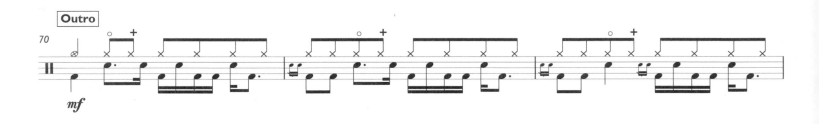

mf

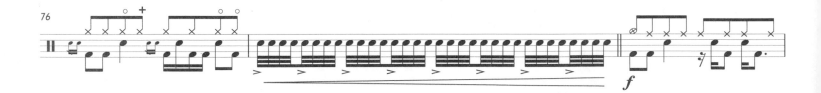

f

KNIVES OUT

Words and Music by
THOMAS YORKE, JONATHAN GREENWOOD,
COLIN GREENWOOD, EDWARD O'BRIEN and PHILIP SELWAY

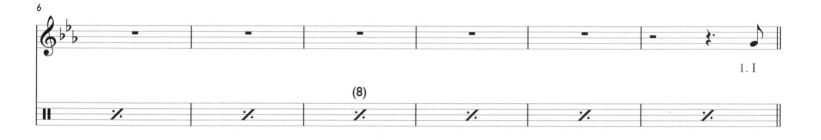

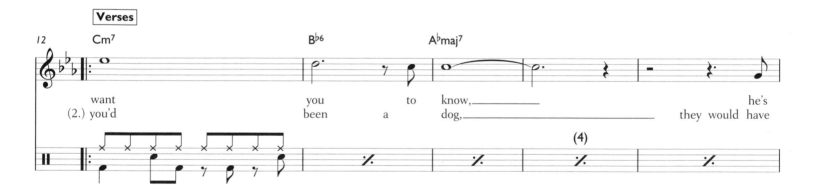

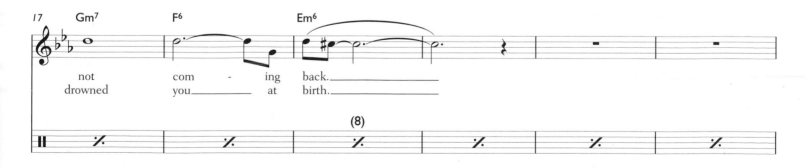

Knives Out - 4 - 1

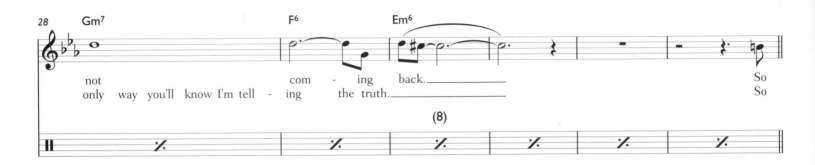

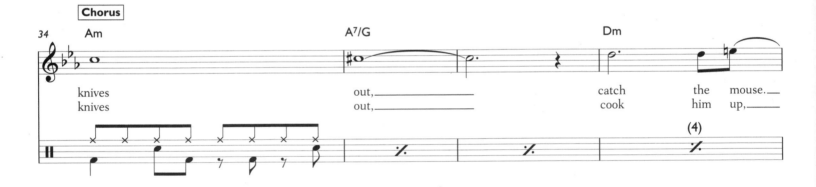

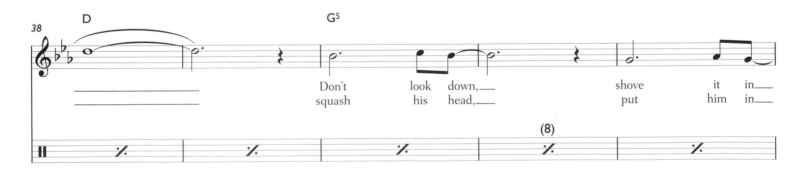

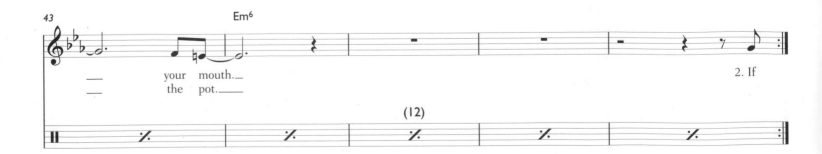

Guitar solo

play x4

3. I

Verse 3

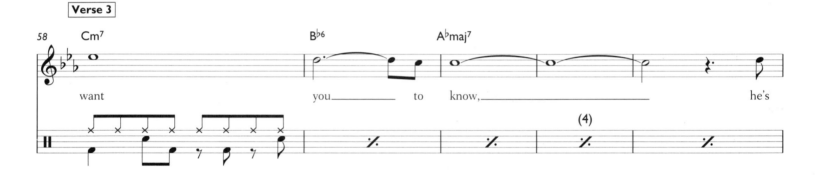

want   you _____ to   know, _____ he's

(4)

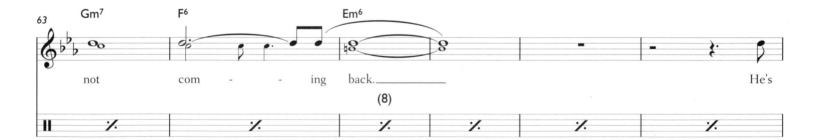

not   com - - ing   back. _____ He's

(8)

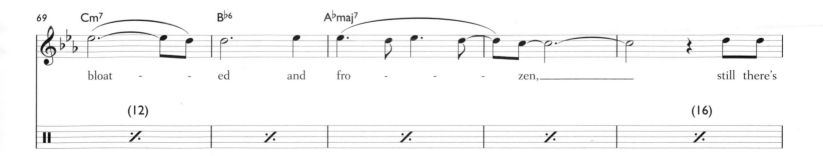

bloat - - ed   and   fro - - - zen, _____ still there's

(12)   (16)

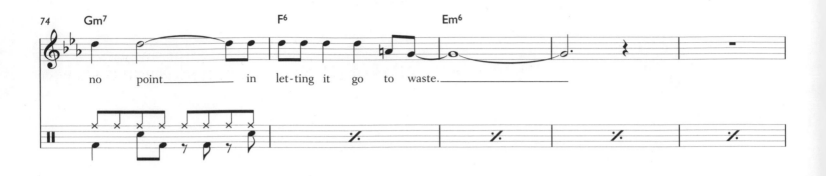

no point_____ in let-ting it go to waste._____

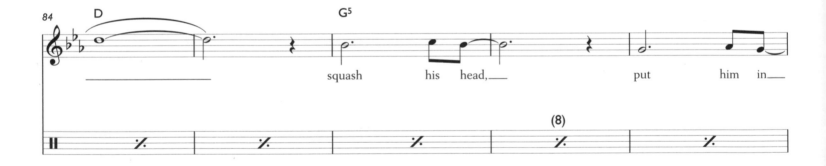

Chorus 2

So knives out,_____ catch the mouse,

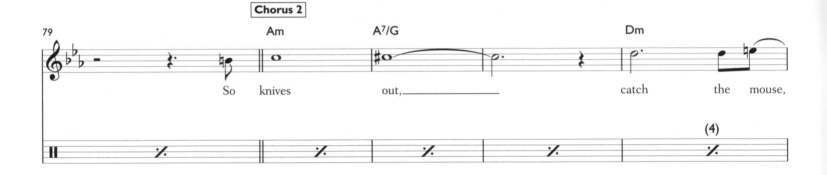

squash his head,___ put him in___

Outro

the pot.___

OPTIMISTIC

Words and Music by
THOMAS YORKE, JONATHAN GREENWOOD,
COLIN GREENWOOD, EDWARD O'BRIEN and PHILIP SELWAY

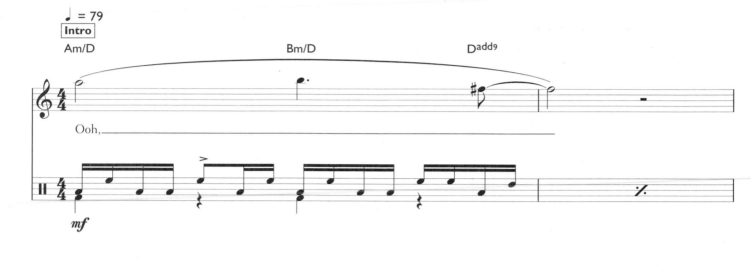

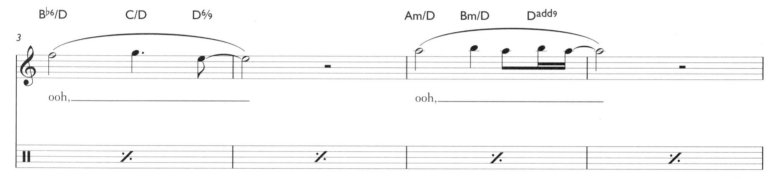

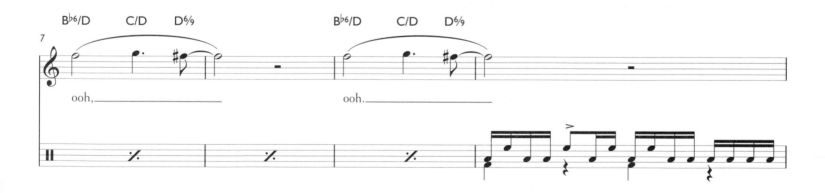

Optimistic - 5 - 1

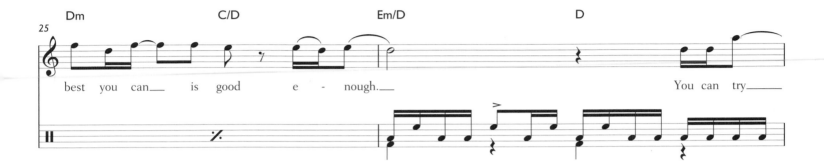

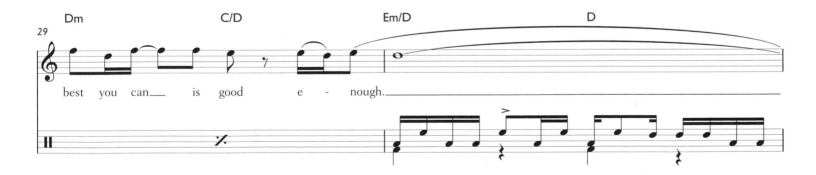

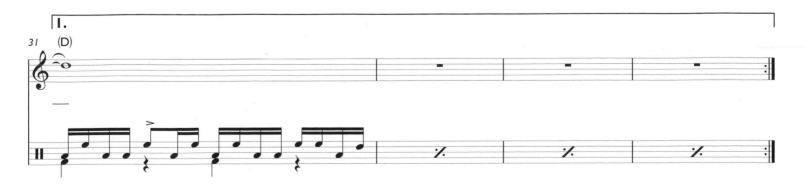

Optimistic - 5 - 3

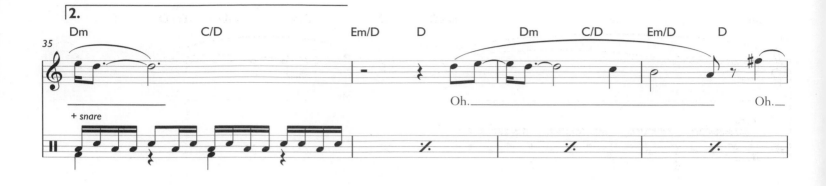

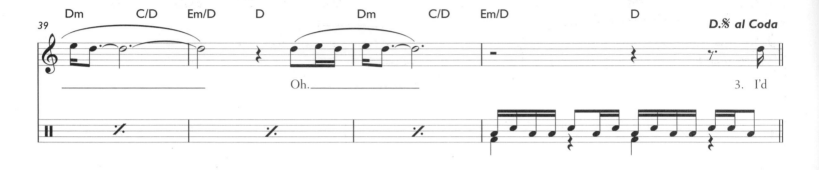

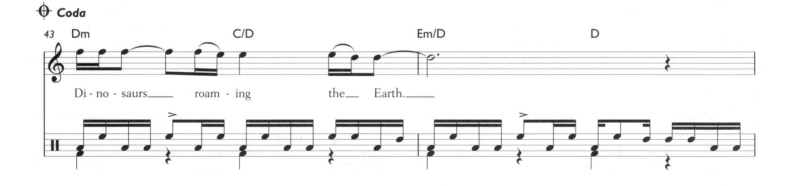

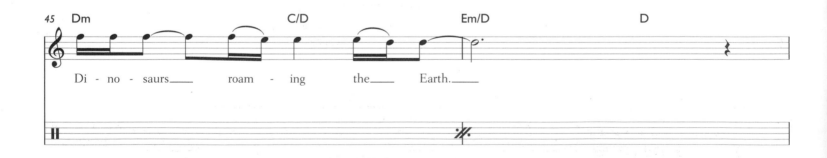

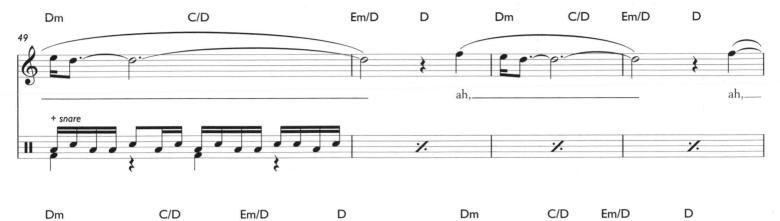

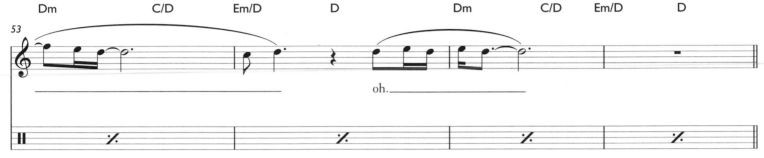

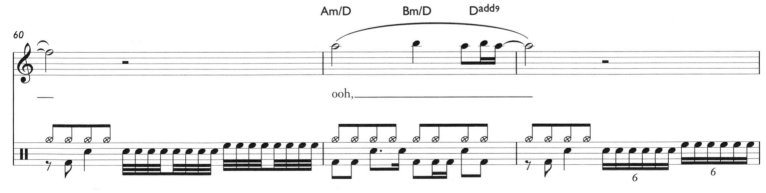

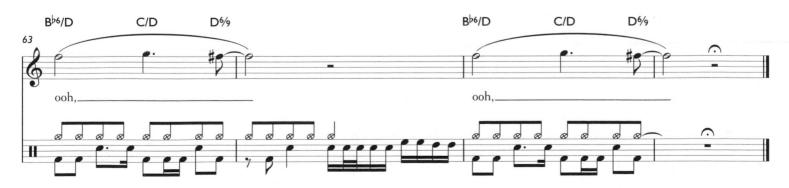

Optimistic - 5 - 5

PARANOID ANDROID

Words and Music by
THOMAS YORKE, JONATHAN GREENWOOD,
COLIN GREENWOOD, EDWARD O'BRIEN and PHILIP SELWAY

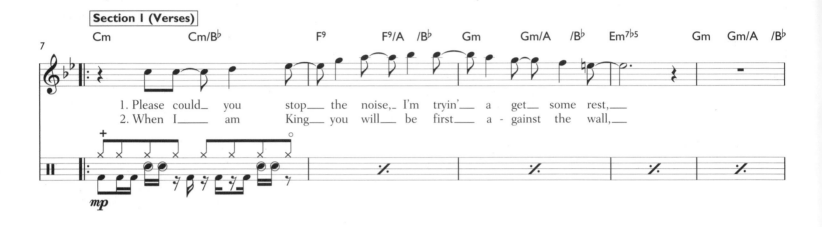

1. Please could you stop the noise, I'm tryin' a get some rest,
2. When I am King you will be first a - gainst the wall,

from all the un - born chick - en voic - es in my head.
with your o - pin - ions which are of no con - se - quence at

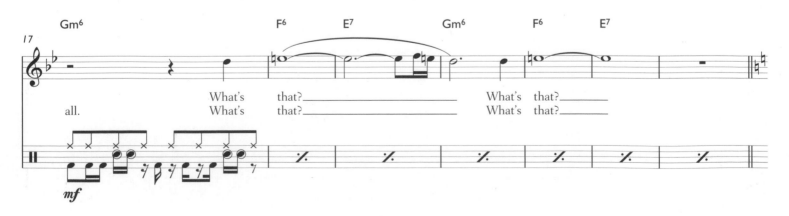

all.
What's that? What's that?
What's that? What's that?

Paranoid Android - 5 - 1

Section 2

24 (32) N.C.

(2°) - bi - tion makes you look pret - ty ug - ly.____ Kick-ing squeal-ing Guc - ci lit-tle pig - gy._

27 (35) C Csus⁴ C A♭ B♭

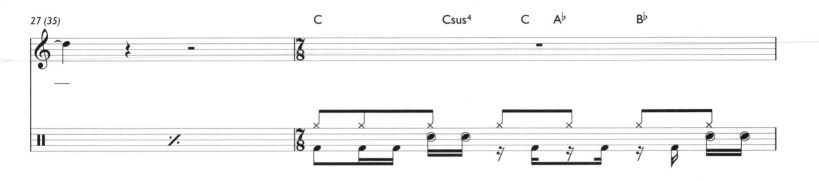

C Csus⁴ C A♭ B♭ C Csus⁴ C A♭ B♭ C Csus⁴ C C♭ B♭ A♭

29 (37)

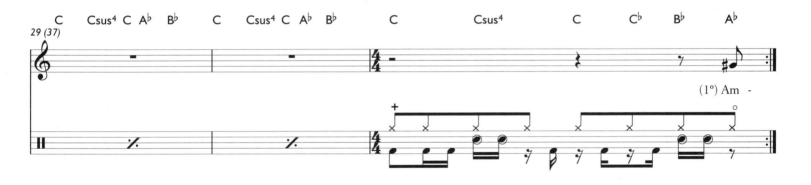

(1°) Am -

Section 3 (Guitar solo)

40

43

_f_

46 _choke_

Section 4

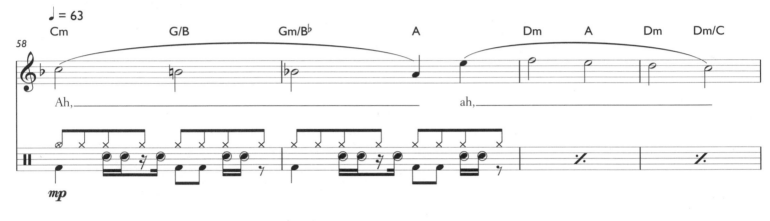

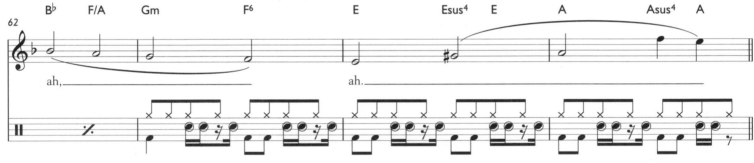

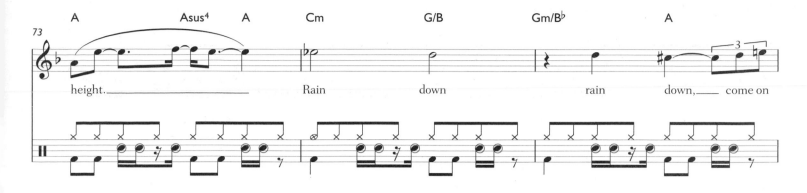

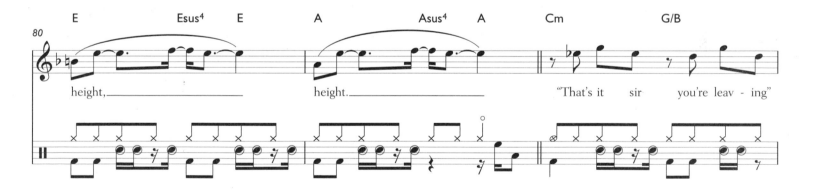

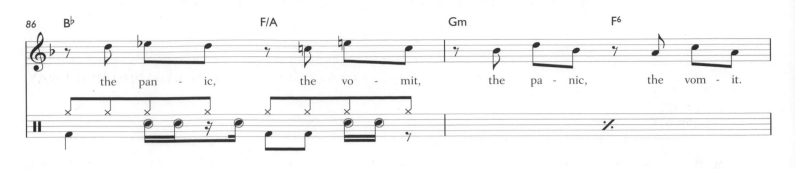

the pan - ic, the vo - mit, the pa - nic, the vom - it.

God loves his child - ren, God loves his child - ren.

Section 5 (Outro)

Tempo I ♩ = 82

f

choke

ff

WEIRD FISHES/ARPEGGI

Words and Music by
THOMAS YORKE, JONATHAN GREENWOOD,
COLIN GREENWOOD, EDWARD O'BRIEN and PHILIP SELWAY

Verses lyrics:

1. In the deep-est oc - ean,   the
2. Why should I___ stay___ here?
(3.) -zy not___ to fol - low,

bot - tom of the sea,   your eyes,___
Why should I_____ where___ you lead.___ stay?
fol - low_____ where___ you lead.___   Your eyes,___

Weird Fishes/Arpeggi - 6 - 1

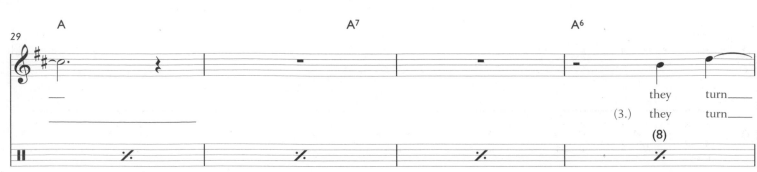

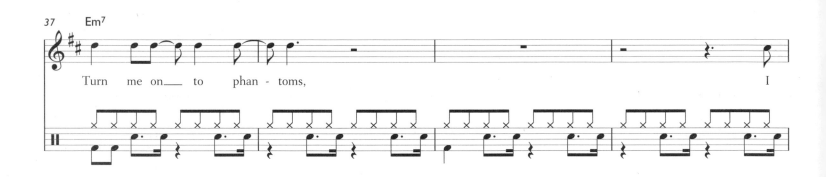

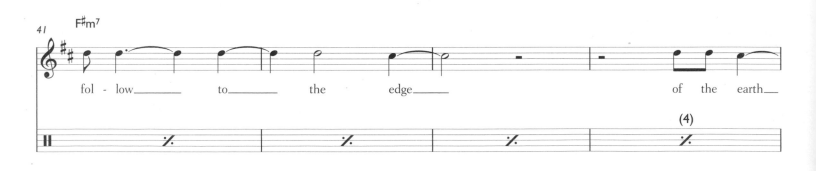

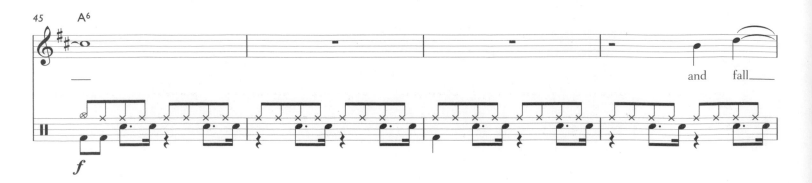

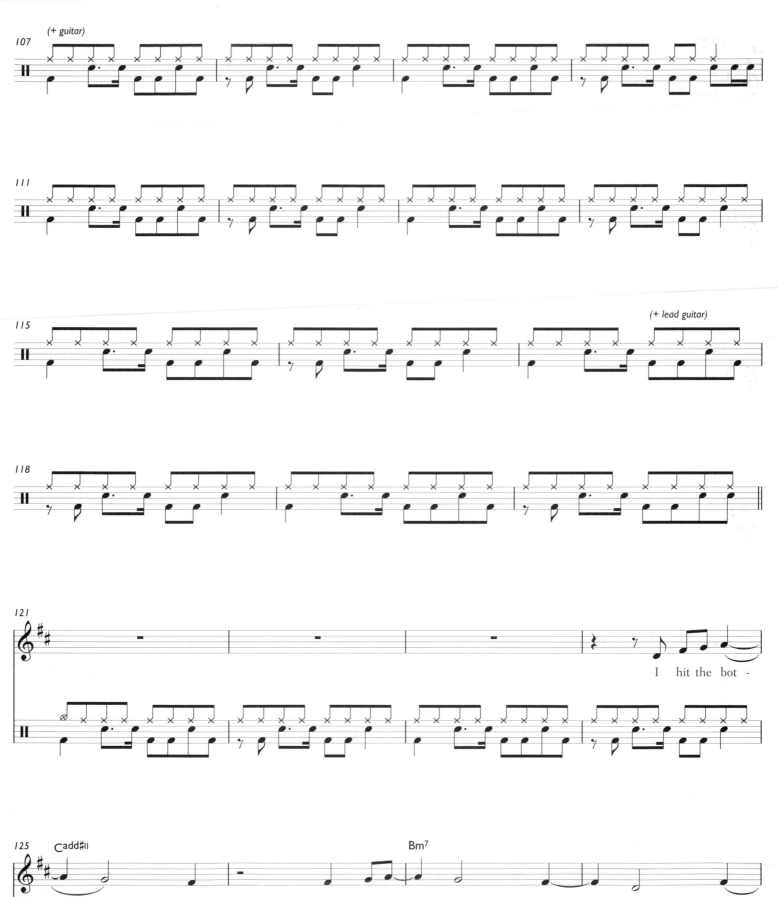

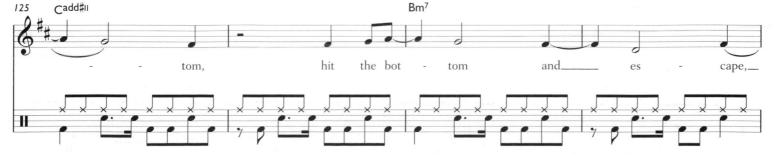

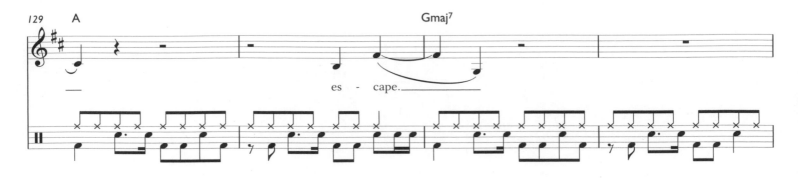

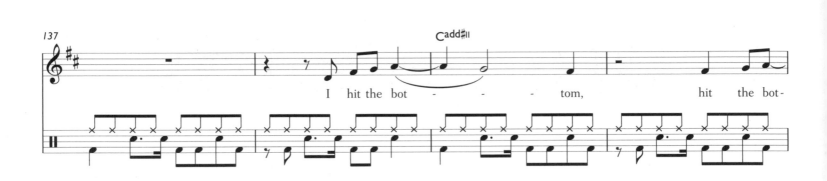

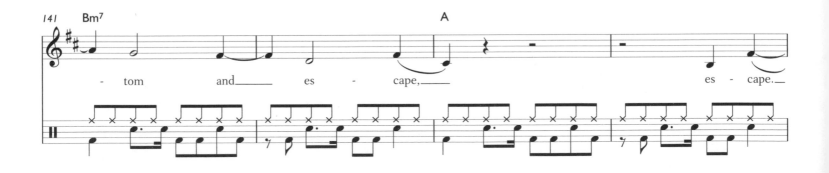

Drum Charts

2+2=5

Words and Music by
THOMAS YORKE, JONATHAN GREENWOOD,
COLIN GREENWOOD, EDWARD O'BRIEN and PHILIP SELWAY

2+2=5 - 2 - 1

ANYONE CAN PLAY GUITAR

Words and Music by
THOMAS YORKE, JONATHAN GREENWOOD,
COLIN GREENWOOD, EDWARD O'BRIEN and PHILIP SELWAY

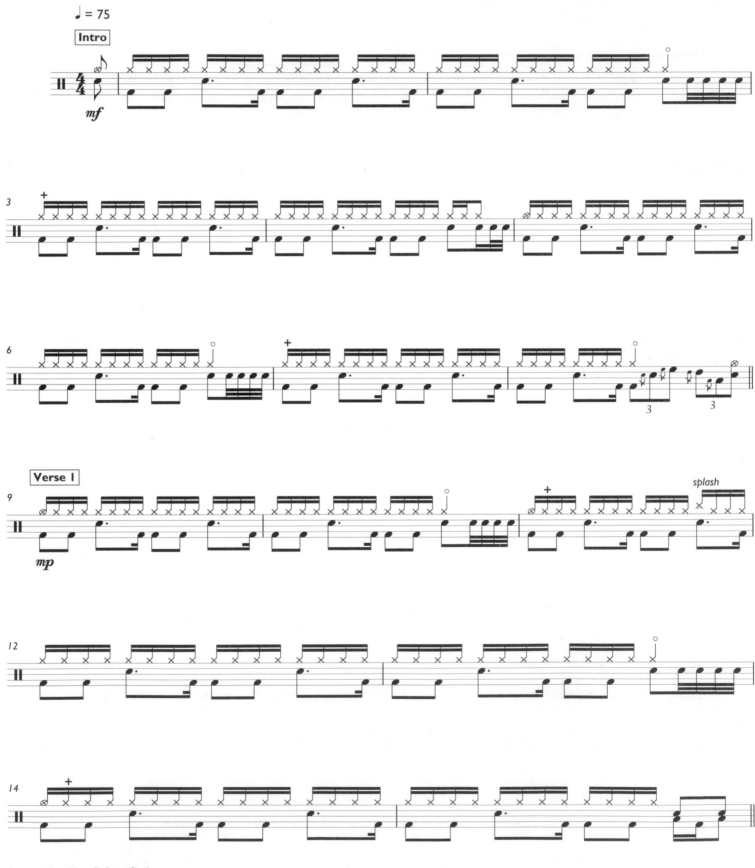

Anyone Can Play Guitar - 3 - 1

double time (♩ = 150)

𝄋 Chorus

Link
tempo I (♩ = 75)   *To Coda* ⊕

Anyone Can Play Guitar - 3 - 2

Verse 2

mp

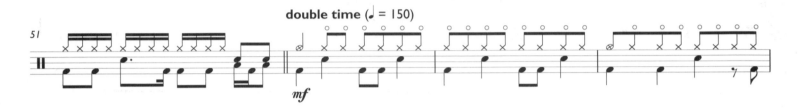

double time (♩ = 150)

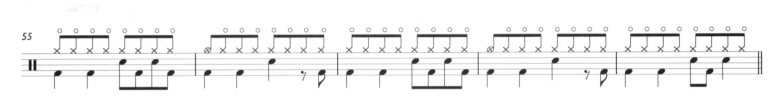

mf

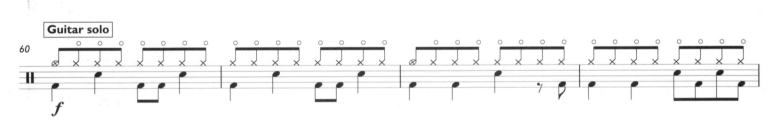

Guitar solo

f

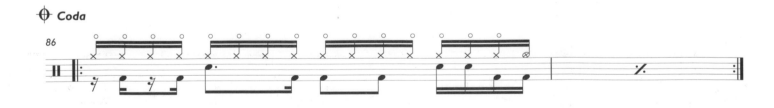

D.𝄋 al Coda

⊕ *Coda*

CREEP

Words and Music by
THOM YORKE, JONATHAN GREENWOOD,
PHILIP SELWAY, COLIN GREENWOOD, EDWARD O'BRIEN,
ALBERT HAMMOND and MIKE HAZELWOOD

Creep - 2 - 1

50

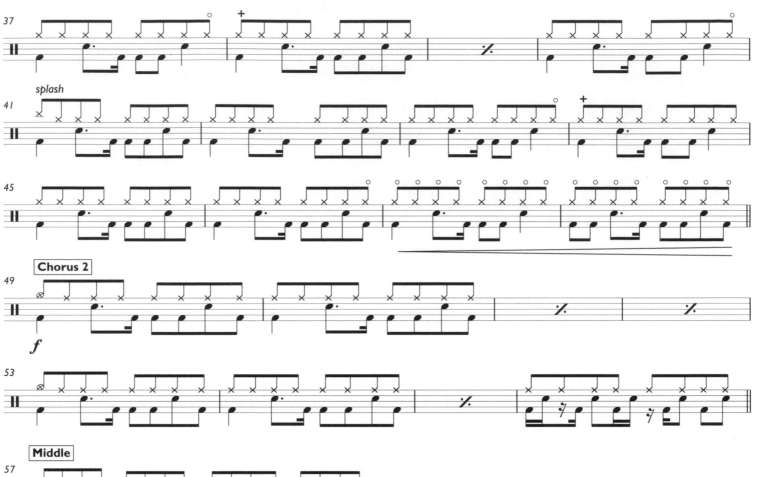

Chorus 2

Middle

Verse 3

Outro chorus

Creep - 2 - 2

JUST

Words and Music by
THOMAS YORKE, JONATHAN GREENWOOD,
COLIN GREENWOOD, EDWARD O'BRIEN and PHILIP SELWAY

Just - 3 - 1

Verse 2

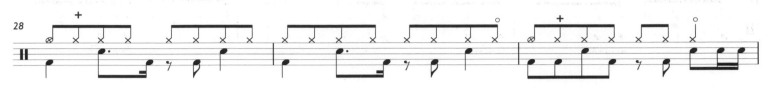

Chorus 2

Guitar solo

Chorus 3

54

f

58

61

64

Outro

70

mf

73

76

78

f

82

KNIVES OUT

Words and Music by
THOMAS YORKE, JONATHAN GREENWOOD,
COLIN GREENWOOD, EDWARD O'BRIEN and PHILIP SELWAY

Knives Out - 2 - 1

OPTIMISTIC

Words and Music by
THOMAS YORKE, JONATHAN GREENWOOD,
COLIN GREENWOOD, EDWARD O'BRIEN and PHILIP SELWAY

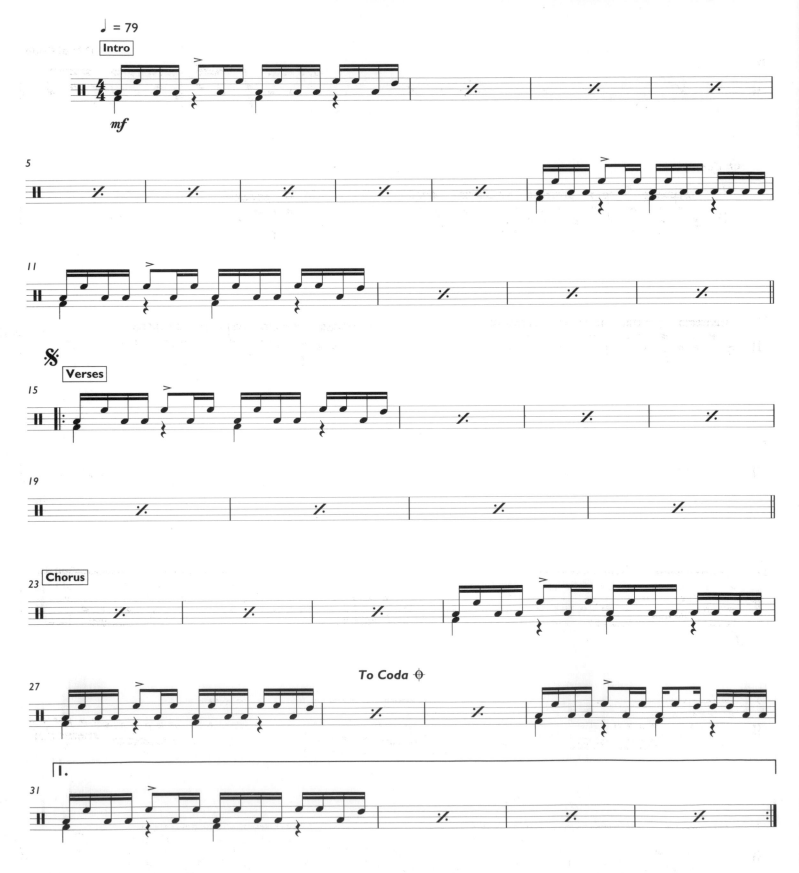

Optimistic - 2 - 1

2.

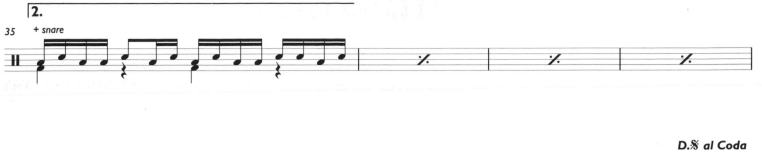

D.% al Coda

⊕ **Coda**

Optimistic - 2 - 2

PARANOID ANDROID

Words and Music by
THOMAS YORKE, JONATHAN GREENWOOD,
COLIN GREENWOOD, EDWARD O'BRIEN and PHILIP SELWAY

Paranoid Android - 3 - 1

Section 3 (Guitar solo)

Section 4

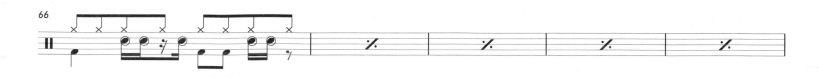

74

79

82

86

Section 5 (Outro)

Tempo I ♩ = 82

90

f

93

97

100
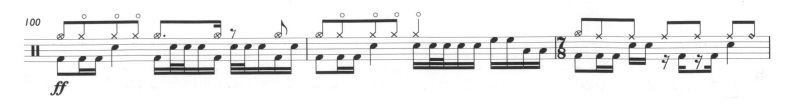

ff

103

WEIRD FISHES/ARPEGGI

Words and Music by
THOMAS YORKE, JONATHAN GREENWOOD,
COLIN GREENWOOD, EDWARD O'BRIEN and PHILIP SELWAY

Weird Fishes/Arpeggi - 3 - 1

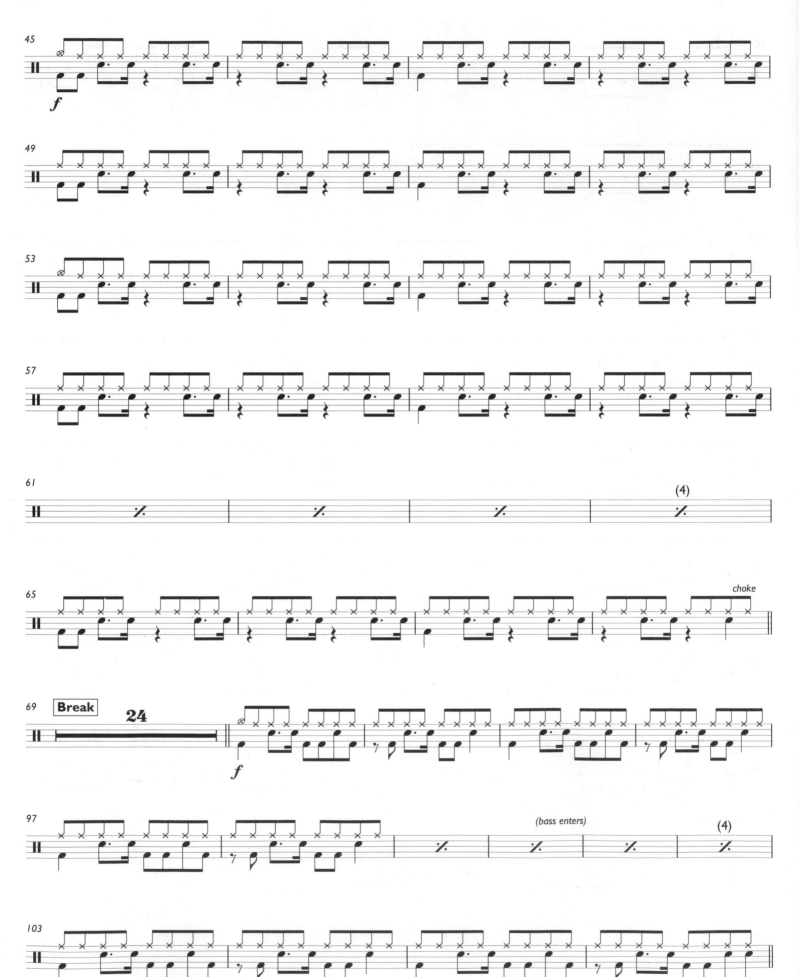

107 (+ guitar)

111

117 (+ lead guitar)

121

125

129

133

137

141

145 let ring

Weird Fishes/Arpeggi - 3 - 3

DRUM KEY

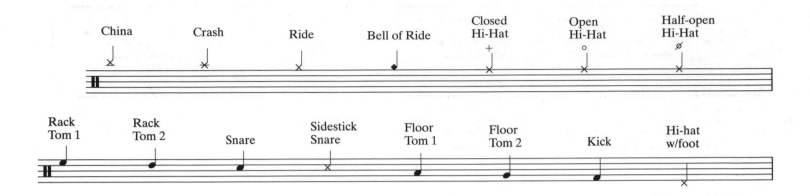